FRED RAMEN

Epidemics
Deadly Diseases
Throughout History

SLEEPING SICKNESS
AND OTHER PARASITIC
TROPICAL DISEASES

The Rosen Publishing Group, Inc.
New York

For Adrienne

Published in 2002 by The Rosen Publishing Group, Inc.
29 East 21st Street, New York, NY 10010

Library of Congress Cataloging-in-Publication Data

Ramen, Fred.
Sleeping sickness and other parasitic tropical diseases / Fred Ramen.
p. cm. — (Epidemics)
Summary: Examines the microscopic world of the parasites that cause sleeping sickness and explains the origin of tropical diseases and their history.
Includes bibliographical references and index.
ISBN 0-8239-3499-3
1. Tropical medicine—Juvenile literature. 2. African trypanoso-miasis—Juvenile literature. 3. Parasitic diseases—Juvenile literature. [1. African trypanosomiasis. 2. Tropical medicine.]
I. Title. II. Series.
RC961.5 .R35 2001
616.9'363—dc21

2001003213

Cover image: Microscopic image of trypanosomes, which cause African sleeping sickness. Multiple parasites and red blood cells are seen in the image.

CONTENTS

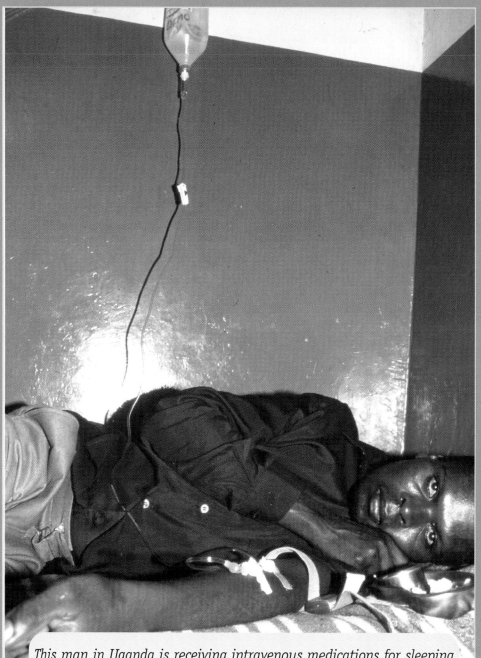

This man in Uganda is receiving intravenous medications for sleeping sickness, which has caused untold suffering throughout the world.

INTRODUCTION

Over 500 years ago, the Portuguese prince Henry the Navigator helped to establish Portugal as a world power. Although he himself probably never traveled beyond sight of the coastline, he helped create a school for training sailors and navigators and paid for several expeditions down the coastline of Africa, venturing into regions few Europeans had ever visited.

Seeking an unknown water route into the African interior, his men sailed up the Gambia River and witnessed a peculiar local custom. Caravans from northern Africa would cross the Sahara to trade with inhabitants of the region around the Gambia. Once they had reached their destination, however, the merchants would lay out their wares in the marketplace without a word and then return to their caravans. The locals would then examine the available goods, also silently, and leave gold coins next to the items they wanted. When the amount of gold was judged to be enough by the people in the caravans, they would take it and the locals would be free to take the goods for which they had paid. This "silent trade" practice may seem bizarre by our standards, but it served an important purpose.

The men of the caravans dared not travel farther south into the dense West African jungle. They feared, quite rightly, for their lives and the lives of their animals. Although they did not know their causes, the deadly diseases of nagana, which affected their animals, and sleeping sickness—both spread by the bite of the tsetse fly—awaited them the farther south they traveled. It is for this reason that they kept their distance from the southerners, not daring to be exposed to them.

PARASITIC DISEASE

Diseases have been around from the very dawn of humankind. Many of the deadly infections that still plague humanity today were present hundreds of thousands of years ago, when the ancestors of today's humans were still living a primitive existence. Far more than any other disaster—war, famine, or earthquake, for example—diseases have shaped the course of human history.

The Black Death

During the fourteenth century, a new disease emerged in Europe, carried westward from Asia by fleas living on the rats that infested the trading ships of the great European merchant houses.

This painting illustrates the suffering wrought by a terrible plague that broke out in the city of Marseilles, France, in 1720.

This disease, the bubonic plague, caused a horrible, painful, and disfiguring death. The victim would have great pus-filled sacs or sores—called buboes—on his or her body. The blackened appearance of some of these sores gave the plague its more famous name: the Black Death.

Over a third of Europe's population would die during the waves of the plague that reoccurred over several centuries. As a result, profound changes transformed European society as people left the fields for the cities to look for work in places where labor had suddenly become necessary. The growth of cities, and the weakening power of nobility (who could not stop workers from leaving their rural estates), inspired the rebirth of learning we now call the Renaissance. This rebirth inspired Europe's exploration of the world, led by wealthy and educated men such as Henry the Navigator. More than all of the countless wars fought by Europeans during this period, the Black Death changed the course of their entire history.

Sleeping Sickness

While Europe was being devastated by the Black Death, the powerful Islamic kingdom of Mali, famous for its fabled king, Mansa Musa (whose pilgrimage to Mecca left all observers stunned by the wealth the king brought with him), had grown into the most powerful territory in western Africa. Yet the wealth and power of Mali could not protect its nobles from a curious affliction that was described by an Arabic historian; one of its kings, Mansa Djata, died of it after suffering for two years. Many of his subjects undoubtedly suffered from the same symptoms and would themselves soon perish. They would experience gradual but increasing drowsiness during the day, which caused them to be barely able to stay awake, yet at the same time, to have an inability to sleep at night. Over time they would find it harder to concentrate and would become depressed or overly emotional.

400 AD
South Americans suffering from Chagas' disease are mummified in the Andes.

1374
Mali's Mansa Djata dies of sleeping sickness.

1700s
Sleeping sickness is observed in slaves taken to the West Indies.

1895
Dr. David Bruce discovers the cause of nagana.

1900
A sleeping sickness epidemic in Uganda kills more than 200,000 people over the course of six years.

Eventually they would become too tired to eat at all and would waste away into a comatose state. Finally, sufferers would slip into a quiet death.

The disease responsible for these symptoms is sleeping sickness, a terrible malady that has afflicted Africa for thousands of years. Like the many diseases that prevented European newcomers from coming to African shores, sleeping sickness was highly contagious to those who had never been exposed to it. For a long time, its source was a mystery, although some Africans suspected a link between it and the bite of the tsetse fly. Today, we know sleeping sickness is caused by parasites that live inside the tsetse fly and are spread when the infected fly bites a person or animal.

1903
Trypanosome infection is confirmed as the cause of sleeping sickness.

1909
Dr. Carlos Chagas discovers the parasite that causes Chagas' disease.

1980s
The civil war in Sudan causes new outbreaks of sleeping sickness.

1906
The sleeping sickness epidemic in Uganda ends.

1920s
New cures for sleeping sickness are discovered.

Sleeping sickness first came to the attention of Europeans during the eighteenth century, when it was observed in slaves who were being transported from Africa to the Americas. In its less severe form, sleeping sickness can infect a person for many years, leaving him or her constantly tired and weak. The fact that some of the slaves suffered from this less severe infection may have been one source of the racist belief of the Europeans that Africans were "lazy."

Not until the end of the nineteenth century was the cause of the disease fully understood. Even today, curing sleeping sickness remains challenging. Sleeping sickness is making a comeback, once again becoming a dangerous health concern in Africa.

Other Parasitic Diseases

Sleeping sickness is not the only parasitic tropical disease. One closely related disease is Chagas' disease of South and Central America. Certain microscopic worms can cause the disfiguring condition known as elephantiasis, which causes the limbs to swell horribly. These worms may also cause a condition known as river blindness. Larger worms infest the waters of tropical regions and can cause serious diseases in human beings. These can include schistosomiasis, which causes blood loss and tissue damage. The bite of another insect— the sand fly—can cause the group of diseases known as leishmaniasis.

Human expansion has led to the spread of parasitic disease.

As the population of humankind has continued to expand globally, settling new lands and disrupting tropical environments such as rain forests, these diseases have once more gained in prominence. In today's high-speed world, where tourists from North America can explore the Amazon River to its source, and where trade between central Africa and the rest of the world can take hours instead of years, these diseases have suddenly become threats to people from all parts of the globe. And in the Tropics themselves, where these illnesses originate, the inhabitants of those regions have had to rededicate themselves to the fight against disease.

But before we can defeat these diseases, we must understand them. The following chapters will take you into the world of these parasites, showing how they attack their human hosts, and what people can do to stop them.

UNWELCOME GUESTS

Sleeping sickness takes a terrible toll on its victims. As the disease progresses, it robs the sufferer of his or her mind, slowly reducing the victim to a comatose skeleton. Long before then, however, the disease will have already caused the person to become forgetful, distracted, and tormented by the inability to sleep at night or stay awake during the day.

Sleeping sickness occurs throughout the central region of Africa, from below the Sahara Desert to the region north of the Cape of Good Hope. Wherever there are bushes or short trees—the preferred habitat of the tsetse fly—the danger of contracting sleeping sickness worsens.

Strains of Sleeping Sickness

Sleeping sickness has three basic forms: East African, West African, and nagana. The first two are diseases of humans, while the last is the form the disease takes in certain animals.

A person who has been bitten by an infected tsetse fly will not show any outward signs for a period of one or two weeks. After that time, he or she will begin to develop a fever that comes and goes and will feel aches and pains. The back of his or her neck will become swollen and painful to the touch; this condition is called Winterbottom's sign and is one of the specific ways that doctors diagnose the disease.

If the person has been infected with the East African form of the disease (also called the Rhodesian form), he or she will soon die unless treated. If, however, he or she has been infected with the West African, or Gambian, form of the disease, the course of the illness will be much longer; he or she should expect a two- to three-year life expectancy. During this time, the infected person will suffer a number of symptoms caused by the destruction of his or her nervous system. These symptoms may include severe headaches, inability to concentrate or take an interest in his or her surroundings, difficulty in walking any faster than a shuffle, tremors, paralysis, sleepiness or drowsiness

Sleeping sickness affects not only humans but cattle as well, enabling the disease to spread to a much greater population over large geographical areas.

during the day, and an inability to sleep at night. The victim usually loses his or her appetite (and is too sleepy to eat during the day, and too distracted to eat at night) and begins to waste away. Eventually, he or she falls into a coma and dies.

Sleeping sickness does not always kill right away, however. Sometimes a person can survive for many years with only a mild form of the disease, although he or she will be continuously carrying the parasites around in his or her body. It is possible for the carriers of the disease to infect others. For instance, if an uninfected tsetse fly bites a carrier, the parasites can be transferred to the fly. After a period of time, this fly will become infected and can spread the disease to the next person it bites.

Sleeping Sickness in Animals

Nagana is the form the disease takes in animals. Many native African animals have a natural immunity to this form of the disease and are not harmed by trypanosomes, the parasites that transmit the disease. However, they can still spread the disease to any uninfected tsetse flies that bite them. These flies can then spread the disease to other animals.

Many animals have no resistance to nagana, which, like sleeping sickness in humans, comes in two types, or strains. Both, however, can infect most domestic animals, especially cattle and horses; related diseases can infect other animals, such as monkeys or pigs. Because of the threat of nagana and other related tropical diseases, it has been almost impossible to bring livestock into regions where the disease is common in Africa. Subsequently, a huge part of the continent—over three million square acres—is entirely off-limits to cattle. And even in regions where cattle are raised, the disease kills three million cows each year.

Health inspectors seeking the cause of an outbreak of sleeping sickness study blood samples in an Angolan village.

A major obstacle to the control and prevention of sleeping sickness is that its deadlier form, the East African or Rhodesian strain, not only affects humans but cattle and antelopes as well. This means that there is a much greater population for the disease to affect in a given area: It can affect not just people but their livestock and wild animals, too. (Scientists call those who can catch a disease—both animals and people—that disease's reservoir; sleeping sickness has both a human and animal reservoir.) Thus, to control the disease in a region, not only must the people be treated, but infected animals must also be eliminated. Usually this means the slaughter of infected animals. In extreme cases, all the animals must be killed to prevent the possibility of the disease remaining undetected in animals that appear healthy.

An example of this kind of extreme treatment occurred in the twentieth century, on the island of São Principe, off the west coast of Africa. A quiet island whose days as a bustling port of the Portuguese colonial empire had long been over, São Principe suddenly found itself infested with sleeping sickness. International commissions arrived to help the islanders develop a plan to end the epidemic. First, they treated what people they could. Then, they slaughtered most of the domestic livestock—cattle and pigs—owned by the islanders. Finally, they ordered the slaughter of the wild pigs and dogs that lived on the island and offered a reward for each wild pig killed. Thousands of animals died, but the epidemic ended.

Chagas' Disease

Another disease that is closely related to sleeping sickness is Chagas' disease, which occurs in South and Central America. Like sleeping sickness, Chagas' disease is caused by parasites that are spread by insects, the vinchuca or barbeiro bugs, also known as the kissing bugs.

Much like sleeping sickness, Chagas' disease can take one of two forms. The first is a short but violent infection (called the acute form of the disease) that may cause fever and inflammation (swelling) of the heart or brain. Most patients survive through four to six weeks of symptoms, although children are more likely to die from the disease in its earliest forms.

However, some patients, even though they have apparently recovered, still harbor the parasites in their bodies. Years later, the second form of the disease, the chronic form, emerges. By now the parasites have invaded the victim's nervous system and internal organs, doing great damage. Often the nerves that the body uses to control its muscles, such as the heart, are damaged to the point that they no longer work. One common problem is that the nerves in the intestine become damaged, preventing the patient from going to the bathroom properly. The colon will begin to enlarge, giving the person a grotesquely swollen belly. Surgery is often the only way to remedy this problem. Without help, the patient will die.

Another common problem among people who have the chronic form of Chagas' disease is damage to the heart. The nerves that regulate heartbeat often become damaged, and the person may need a pacemaker in order to live a normal, active life. Often the heart will become dangerously enlarged. Patients with heart damage frequently become bedridden, unable to do many activities because they tire so easily. In some of the mountainous regions of South America, such as Bolivia, people with chronic Chagas' disease are further hampered by the region's extreme altitude, where the air is thin and the victims' hearts and lungs have to work much harder than at lower elevations.

Although the cause of Chagas' disease was only discovered early in the twentieth century (only then did it become clear to medical professionals that it was one disease that took many forms), it has been around for a very long time. The earliest known evidence of the disease is the mummified bodies of an ancient South American culture called the Wankari. These 1,600-year-old mummies display signs such as enlarged intestines and hearts that indicate they had Chagas' disease. Scientists now believe that the illness has been infecting humans for at least 6,000 years.

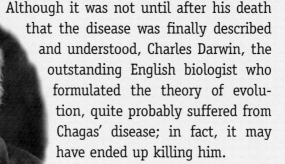

Charles Darwin

Although it was not until after his death that the disease was finally described and understood, Charles Darwin, the outstanding English biologist who formulated the theory of evolution, quite probably suffered from Chagas' disease; in fact, it may have ended up killing him.

While in his twenties, Darwin made a trip aboard the British ship H.M.S. *Beagle* to South America. His observations there would be key to his theory that every life-form develops from common ancestors, evolving (changing) in order to better adapt to its environment. Yet it was also during this time that he encountered the vinchuca bug. He allowed one to bite his hand and draw blood so he could study its feeding habits. Within a few years of this meeting with the kissing bug, Darwin developed symptoms such as fever, fatigue, and depression that plagued him at varying periods for the rest of his life. These symptoms did not seem to have any obvious cause, but came and went with varying frequencies. When Darwin died in 1882 at the age of seventy-two, he suffered from heart damage, which, as we have seen, is frequently a result of the chronic form of Chagas' disease.

Although it cannot be known with certainty that Darwin did indeed have Chagas' disease, his symptoms, ultimate cause of death, and the fact that he encountered the vinchuca bug while in South America make it a good bet that it was the malady that haunted him for many years.

Other Parasitic Tropical Diseases

Sleeping sickness and Chagas' disease are far from the only parasitic diseases people can catch in the Tropics. One particularly horrible disease that is the result of a parasite similar to the one that causes sleeping sickness is leishmaniasis. This disease is spread by the bite of the sand fly, and it occurs all around the world. It is most common, however, in the Mediterranean region, Africa, Asia, and Latin America.

Leishmaniasis can take two different forms. Visceral leishmaniasis affects the nervous system and the internal organs, especially the liver, spleen, and bone marrow. People who have this form of the disease suffer from fever, loss of weight, and an enlarged liver and spleen. Unless treated, this form of the disease is usually fatal. However, it can take years for the symptoms to occur.

The second form of the disease, cutaneous leishmaniasis, causes open sores on the skin. These can result in ugly scars. It is possible for the disease to spread to the mouth and nose; if this happens, severe damage to the lips, throat, roof of the mouth, or voice box can occur. Treatment is complicated by the fact that this form of the disease (also called mucocutaneous leishmaniasis) may not develop until years after a sore caused by the cutaneous form of the disease has healed.

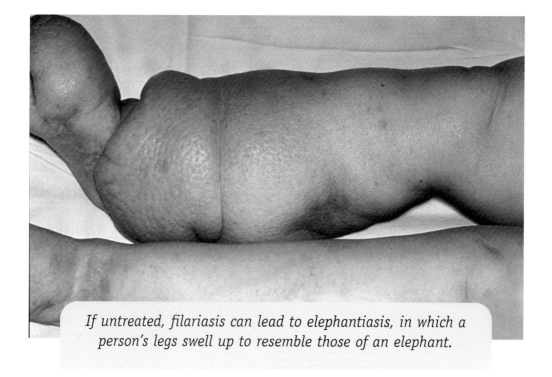

If untreated, filariasis can lead to elephantiasis, in which a person's legs swell up to resemble those of an elephant.

Tiny worms invading the body can cause several serious diseases. Two of the most dangerous are filariasis and schistosomiasis.

Mosquitoes carry filariasis parasites. A human bitten by an infected insect soon becomes a host, or home, to the worms. In one form of filariasis, the worms mostly live in the lymph nodes, especially those responsible for draining the legs. (The lymphatic system acts as the body's "sewer system," draining fluid and dead cells from the body and collecting this useless matter together so that it can be expelled.) Over time, the lymph nodes and channels become damaged and hardened, resulting in poor circulation to the legs and lower regions of the body. If not treated, this can lead to the extreme condition called elephantiasis, where the legs swell up grotesquely, making them resemble the legs of an elephant.

Another form of filariasis is called river blindness. In this form of the disease, the worms travel beneath the skin, leaving scars where they pass. If they reach the eyes, this scarring can eventually blind the infected person, which is how the disease got its name.

Schistosomiasis is a tropical disease caused by worms known as blood flukes. These worms infect snails that live in streams and other bodies of water

This is an image of the intestinal blood flukes called Schistosoma mansoni, *which cause schistosomiasis.*

in the Tropics. People who swim or bathe in water inhabited by the infected snails may catch the disease themselves. Once inside the body, the blood flukes grow and begin to lay eggs in the walls of the internal organs. This can cause damage to those organs and result in kidney stones, serious liver damage, and even damage of the brain. The flukes' eggs can invade practically any part of the body. If not treated, the damage to the body's internal organs can become severe enough to kill the host (the person suffering from the disease).

In this chapter, we have investigated many different kinds of tropical, parasitic diseases. However, to better understand how these diseases actually develop—which is very important if we are to have any hope of curing and controlling them—we must actually enter the microscopic world of the parasites to examine their life cycle and what makes them so deadly. We must meet the killers themselves.

3

MEET THE KILLERS

All infectious diseases are caused by parasites—creatures that rely on another organism, plant or animal, to provide them with the food they need. Many parasites also rely on the organism they live in—called the host organism—to help them develop. However, there are important differences in the kinds of parasites and the methods in which they are treated.

Viruses

The smallest of all the parasites are the viruses. Viruses cannot reproduce themselves. They first must enter a cell of their host. Once inside that cell, the virus "hijacks" the cell's own natural replication process and uses it to make copies of itself. Eventually, the host cell is destroyed, and the new viruses spread to other cells inside the host. Viruses are much smaller than living cells and are invisible under most microscopes. It took a long time before scientists even realized they existed, since the primitive microscopes they were using could find no trace of the tiny virus cells. Viruses are not destroyed by antibiotics and are therefore much harder to treat than infections caused by bacteria. Viruses are the cause of AIDS, influenza (the flu), the common cold, and many other diseases.

Bacteria

Bacteria are the next kind of parasite that can invade other organisms. Bacteria are single-celled creatures that use the same nutrients as the host in which they are living. As the infection grows and multiplies, it can damage the cells of the host. Many bacteria produce poisonous chemicals that can also damage the host. Antibiotics can kill bacteria and are the drugs of choice for treating bacterial infections. Bacteria are the cause of tuberculosis, leprosy, and other diseases, and were responsible for the bubonic plague (Black Death).

When people speak about parasitic infections, they usually mean infections caused by creatures that are more complex than bacteria or viruses. Although many parasites, such as those that cause malaria or sleeping sickness, are microscopic, others can be much larger, such as the intestinal parasite called a tapeworm, which can grow to be several feet long.

The parasites discussed in this book infect more than just people; all of them also infect animals, generally not damaging them, but instead using them to infect other animals. These animals are called carriers of the disease; for example, the tsetse fly is the carrier of sleeping sickness. Knowing which animal carries which disease is important in combating the spread of that disease.

The Microscopic World

Of the twenty-one identified species of tsetse fly, only two are known carriers of sleeping sickness; one spreads the West African strain, and the other spreads the East African strain, as well as nagana. These two species both carry within their bodies the microscopic parasites known as trypanosomes, which cause sleeping sickness.

This is a microscopic image of the head of a tsetse fly.

Sleeping sickness and nagana are both carried by the tsetse fly, a species native to Africa. Although related to the common housefly, tsetse flies are larger, sometimes over half an inch long. They are dark brown or yellowish brown, and have a stiff, piercing mouth that is used to suck blood from other animals.

Unlike many insects, the tsetse fly does not lay eggs. Rather, a single egg hatches inside the mother, held in a special compartment in her body; the larva or young fly that is hatched is then extruded from the mother, almost as if she were giving birth. The larva is deposited on the ground and immediately burrows into the dirt; several weeks later, it will emerge as an adult tsetse fly.

Tsetse flies live about one to three months. Drinking blood is extremely important to them, and they do so almost daily. Without a proper blood meal, the female will not be able to produce a healthy larva. Tsetse flies generally inhabit wooded areas, although they will chase prey into the open. They generally feed during the hottest parts of the day and stop attacking after sunset.

The Trypanosome Parasite

Trypanosomes are single-celled creatures that can move about freely. Their name, which means "auger-body," comes from the twisting way they move. (It reminded early observers of the way an auger, or drill, moved.) About twenty species of this parasite are known to exist, but only two types cause disease in humans. Several other types cause diseases in livestock, such as the species that causes nagana in Africa.

A trypanosome is a transparent, snakelike organism about twice as large as a red blood cell. One end is somewhat pointed, and the other ends in a threadlike lash called a flagellum. By rapidly beating the flagellum, the trypanosome can propel itself through the bloodstream of its host. Running down each side of the animal is a thin wing, or fin, which wiggles as it moves.

The trypanosomes that cause sleeping sickness and nagana have a complex life cycle that involves both a mammal and an insect host. The trypanosomes appear in the body of a mammal that has been previously infected. When a tsetse fly sucks blood from this infected animal, it also ingests some of the trypanosomes. At this stage of development, they are rounded cells called amastigotes. They multiply inside the stomach of the fly by splitting themselves into two smaller trypanosomes, a process called binary division. At this point in their life cycle, the trypanosomes are not infectious; they must first spend a period of time in the fly's gut, where they become fatter and take on the shape just described, called a promastigote. They can now move toward the fly's salivary glands. It is in this way that when the fly next bites an animal, it will pass the trypanosomes into that animal's bloodstream. That animal will become infected and will be capable of spreading the disease to other flies that bite it.

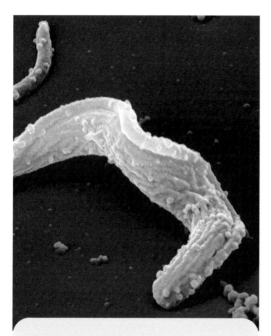

The trypanosome is a tiny, transparent, snakelike organism that wriggles throughout the bloodstream of its host.

Sleeping sickness is caused by one species of trypanosome, although there are two subspecies of this species, each of which produces a different strain of the disease. When the trypanosomes initially invade the bloodstream of a person, the body's immune system immediately attacks them. Unfortunately, trypanosomes are tricky and unpredictable. The cells of the human body that attack invaders do so by recognizing the structure of the outer boundary, or cell wall, of invading cells. But trypanosomes can actually change the composition of their cell walls just enough so that the body cannot recognize them immediately. It takes time for the body's defenses to identify the new configuration, and by the time they do so, the trypanosomes may have switched to another configuration. It is in this way that they can continually stress the body's defenses, gradually wearing a person out.

The more vicious East African strain of the disease kills its host fairly rapidly, usually within a few weeks. But in the West African strain, after the initial period of invasion, the trypanosomes proceed to enter the nervous system and brain of their victim. The damage they do there results in the familiar symptoms of sleeping sickness, especially the daytime drowsiness that gives the disease its name.

The Vinchuca Parasite, or Kissing Bug

Like sleeping sickness, Chagas' disease is carried and transmitted by insects. The culprit in this case is a rather nasty looking bug called *Triatoma infestans*, the kissing bug, also known as the vinchuca or barbeiro. (The latter name, which means "barber," comes from the bloody wounds left on the faces of its victims, reminding people of the nicks a barber might accidentally cause when shaving someone's face.)

The predatory habits of the kissing bug are practically the opposite of the tsetse. Vinchucas hide during the day within the cracks of buildings. At night they emerge, crawling from their hiding spots to attack their sleeping victims. Mosquito netting offers little protection because the bugs are superb crawlers and can sneak in under the fabric.

The vinchuca goes through five life stages, changing from a tiny insect about the size of a flea to a big bug about an inch long. In the fifth and final stage, it grows wings and is able to fly. It is during this period that it breeds and lays eggs.

Because of anesthetic elements in the saliva of the vinchuca, its bite is not painful. It is a common, if not disgusting, occurrence for a sleeper to suddenly awake in the middle of an attack and smash the insect, splattering the area with blood the insect has swallowed. Each bug can ingest more than its own weight in blood, and each must make at least one blood meal during each stage of its life.

The parasite that causes Chagas' disease is another trypanosome, a close relative to the parasite that causes sleeping sickness and nagana. As in the case of sleeping sickness, the trypanosome must spend some time developing inside the insect that carries it. However, it is not transmitted by the bite of the vinchuca. Rather, while the bug is sucking blood from

Chagas' disease is carried and transmitted by the kissing bug, also known as the vinchuca or barbeiro.

its victim, it will defecate. The waste matter it expels contains the trypanosomes, which can then enter the body through the wound left by the bug's attack. If this is near the victim's eyes, as it frequently is, the victim may develop a swelling around one eye called Romana's sign, which is used by doctors to diagnose acute Chagas' disease.

Like sleeping sickness, Chagas' disease can be either acute, meaning that it does severe damage in a short time (like the East African strain of sleeping sickness), or chronic, meaning that it does less damage but lasts a longer time (like the West African strain of sleeping sickness). However, unlike sleeping sickness, both kinds of Chagas' disease are caused by the same parasite. The acute stage lasts about a month and does not usually kill healthy adults. Young children are those most likely to die from the disease in this stage.

Many people never have any further symptoms from the disease, except perhaps exhaustion; indeed, they gain a partial immunity from further infection because they are already carrying the trypanosomes in their bodies. In about one-fourth of the cases, however, the chronic form of the disease emerges after several years. Like sleeping sickness, the trypanosome that causes Chagas' disease attacks the nervous system; it prefers the control centers for various muscles, especially those of the intestine and the heart, as we have seen. These complications frequently result in the death of the patient, though often many years after he or she was initially infected, as was the suspected case with Charles Darwin.

The Leishmaniasis Parasite

As seen in sleeping sickness and Chagas' disease, leishmaniasis is caused by a single-celled organism with a flagellum. Its life cycle is very similar to the trypanosome infections as well: It spends a period of development in the digestive tract of an insect, where it changes from a rounded amastigote to an elongated promastigote.

The carrier of the leishmaniasis parasite is the sand fly. Unlike the carriers of sleeping sickness or Chagas' disease, the sand fly is much smaller, less than a quarter of an inch long. These flies spend a period of time living in the water before they grow wings and take to the air to breed and feed.

Nematode and Trematode Parasitic Worms

Filariasis and schistosomiasis diseases differ from the trypanosome and leishmaniasis diseases mainly in that the parasites involved—worms—are more complex and much larger creatures than the single-celled parasites that cause those diseases, although they are still small.

In filariasis, the female worm (which scientists call a nematode) gives birth to tiny embryos, called microfilariae. These embryos live in the bloodstream of the host animal and are sucked in, along with blood, by mosquitoes. Inside the mosquito, they develop into worms and move into the insect's salivary glands, where they can be spread by the mosquito.

Schistosomiasis worms are flatworms known as trematodes. Their life cycle is slightly more complex than that of filariasis worms.

The carriers of the schistosomiasis worm are several species of snails. However, the worms reproduce inside the animals they infect, which include humans.

The female trematode (also called a fluke worm) will lay from 300 to 3,500 eggs into the blood. Eventually these eggs make their way into the intestine or bladder of the infected animal, and are flushed from the body the next time the animal expels waste.

A medical researcher examines clues to an outbreak of sleeping sickness.

If the waste matter expelled from the animal reaches water, the eggs hatch and release microscopic larvae coated in special hairlike structures called cilia. By beating these hairs like oars on a boat, the larvae are able to move around the water until they find a snail host. They enter the snail and after a period of time develop into fork-tailed creatures called cercariae. Emerging from the snail, they swim around until they find a mammal. They then enter its skin, drop their tails, and develop inside the mammal's bloodstream. Feeding on the host's nutrients, they grow larger; female flukes can be from half an inch to an inch long. In time, the female begins to lay eggs, and the cycle starts over again. However, as we have seen, laying eggs in the organs of the host can cause extreme damage. The worms can live for twenty years, continuing to hurt the host during its life span.

Knowing about the life cycles of the various parasites that cause tropical diseases has helped scientists combat those diseases. By understanding how each parasite grows and develops, scientists can look for weak spots in its defenses, such as points where its growth can be disrupted, and the chain of infection and disease can be broken. Understanding which animals act as carriers is also vital because without controlling the carrier animals, attempts to prevent or destroy the disease will be futile. In the next chapter, we will examine how doctors and scientists have battled against the two major trypanosome infections—sleeping sickness and Chagas' disease—and which drugs can be used to cure the other fearsome parasitic diseases we have discussed.

THE FIGHT AGAINST TROPICAL DISEASES

4

For most of human history, the causes of diseases were not understood. People thought they became sick because of magic spells, or the displeasure of the gods, or because of bad things they did or ate. Many diseases that we now know are caused by infections, such as tuberculosis, were believed to be genetically inherited. Only in the nineteenth century did the tools of science develop, making it possible to identify the causes and effects of many illnesses.

Even during this period, some people refused to believe that a microscopic organism could cause disease in a person. During the early part of the nineteenth century, many people still believed that "bad air" could cause disease.

In fact, the parasitic disease malaria, which is spread by mosquitoes, takes its name from the Italian words for "bad air." Only through the research of such brilliant scientists as Louis Pasteur was it established that bacteria and other parasites *do* infect people, giving them diseases, and that it is possible for these diseases to spread to others in a variety of ways.

The British Encounter Sleeping Sickness

As the Europeans began to understand diseases and even discover cures for them, they were finally able to explore the central jungle regions of Africa and South America. In Africa, the British gained control over many of the regions afflicted with East African sleeping sickness and nagana—South Africa, Zimbabwe (then known as Rhodesia), Kenya, and Uganda. These two diseases were soon a major concern for the British.

Both diseases became epidemics. One of the many reasons for the rapid development of sleeping sickness in these areas was that they were newly settled by the British people who were totally unaware of (and previously unexposed to) the parasites carrying the disease. When they expanded into the jungle, the British were in daily contact with the tsetse flies, causing the disease to spread rapidly. And because people from many different regions were brought together to work on projects such as building railroads, the disease spread even more swiftly than ever before. Ironically, because the British did not allow the Africans to move around as freely as they had previously, preferring them to stay in one place where they could be watched, villages were soon stricken by sleeping sickness as the flies moved into their region. (In the old days, the people would have moved to a new location; now they were forced to suffer the full force of the disease.)

Dr. David Bruce identified a trypanosome as the cause of nagana.

Nagana was also an enormous problem for the British because it affected their livestock, especially cattle and horses. In 1895, Dr. David Bruce, a British doctor stationed in South Africa, succeeded in identifying the cause of the disease as a trypanosome and indicated that he believed it was spread by the tsetse fly, as the Zulus of the region also believed. Subsequent experiments confirmed this suspicion. The next question to be addressed was whether or not sleeping sickness, which had many of the same symptoms as nagana, was also caused by a trypanosome.

Albert Castellani found that a trypanosome caused filariasis.

Ironically, an expedition to Africa that tried to prove that sleeping sickness was caused by one of the worms that caused filariasis actually managed to prove that a trypanosome was the true culprit. An Italian doctor working for the British government, Albert Castellani, made this discovery in 1903, the same year that David Bruce confirmed that the tsetse fly spread the disease to humans.

Chagas' disease is somewhat unusual in that the cause of the disease was actually discovered before doctors realized that it definitely caused a disease. Carlos Chagas (1879–1934) was an outstanding Brazilian doctor and researcher. As a young man, he did field work in the Brazilian rain forest, helping to care for the impoverished people of the region.

In 1908, he was asked to examine the people of Lassance, a village of railroad workers in central Brazil. Many of the people were dying of heart problems without any apparent cause. After eliminating syphilis and malaria as possible causes, Chagas began to study the insects of the region to see if they were spreading some unknown disease. In the guts of vinchucas he found a trypanosome that closely resembled the trypanosome that caused sleeping sickness. Next, he examined people in the region for signs of the trypanosomes and found them in a young girl who died of what we now call the acute stage of Chagas' disease. Having proven that the trypanosomes infected humans, he proceeded to test animals and found monkeys could also die of the disease. He now had the evidence that he needed to prove that the mysterious disease of Lassance was caused by the new trypanosome he had discovered. In honor of this remarkable medical detective work, the disease was named after him.

Searching for Solutions

As early as 1895, Bruce had tried treating horses infected with nagana with the poisonous metal arsenic. He had some success in curing animals, but he could not prevent their further infection. Later scientists, including the renowned German bacteriologist Robert Koch, who had earlier discovered the bacteria that causes tuberculosis, used a drug called atoxyl, which was derived from arsenic. Unfortunately, the drug had severe side effects, including blindness, and had to be administered in doses that were too low to completely eradicate the trypanosomes. Later advances found drugs that were more effective but not as dangerous.

Today, the main treatment for sleeping sickness in its early stages is the drug suramin. For West African sleeping sickness, pentamidine or eflornithine is prescribed; for East African sleeping sickness, eflornithine or melarsoprol are used. The latter is given when the disease has begun attacking the brain. Unfortunately, every drug mentioned here is poisonous to some degree, and the injections are painful. Melarsoprol is especially severe; patients often must be forced to take an injection of this drug. Melarsoprol can also cause an allergic reaction in some patients, compelling doctors to use other medications to treat them.

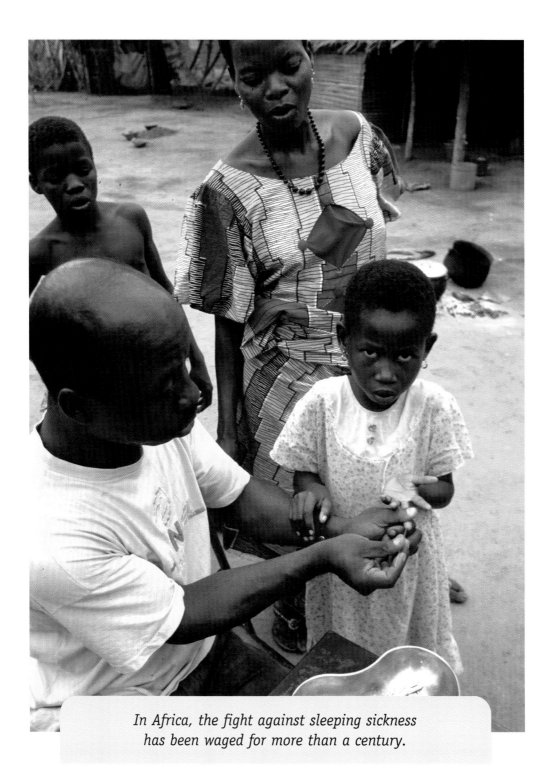

In Africa, the fight against sleeping sickness
has been waged for more than a century.

In its early and acute stages, the drugs nifurtimox and benznidazole can control Chagas' disease. However, they do not work with patients suffering from the chronic effects of the disease. The only things that can be done to help these people are to relieve their symptoms, often by surgically removing damaged organs.

However, advances continue to be made in drug therapies, and all of the diseases we have discussed have at least a partial treatment. As with all diseases, the earlier they are detected, the more effective the treatment is. Today, researchers are searching to find vaccines for these illnesses, which would give people immunity from the afflictions.

Treating a person with drugs, however, is only one side of the task of destroying these diseases. What good does it do to cure a person if the person lives in an area where he or she can catch the disease again and again? For this reason, an important aspect of combating these parasitic diseases is destroying their carriers.

In Africa, the battle against sleeping sickness has been going on for more than a century. Once the vital connection between the trypanosomes and the tsetse flies was understood, plans were made to break this cycle and eradicate the disease once and for all. This was a vital concern during the early days of the twentieth century, as a sleeping sickness epidemic in Uganda, from 1900 to 1906, killed more than 200,000 people.

A sanitary engineer sprays DDT powder to kill plague-carrying fleas near Oshakati in northern Namibia.

There was also a very practical reason to combat sleeping sickness (and nagana): much of the most fertile land in Africa was off-limits to both people and livestock.

During the Ugandan sleeping sickness epidemic, one technique used was to evacuate the population to higher ground that was free of tsetse infestation. New villages were constructed with better sanitation, resulting in a great reduction of the disease. Similar techniques have been used in South America to combat Chagas' disease, although the goal is to make people's homes bugproof by sealing cracks that the vinchucas like to live in, rather than move individuals to higher ground.

Another technique used to fight sleeping sickness is to destroy the natural habitat of the tsetse fly. By burning down the trees they live in, it is possible to drive the tsetse out of a region entirely. This was done for many years in British East Africa. Attempts have also been made to kill the animals that can be infected with the trypanosomes without catching the disease itself, but many people object to this.

During the 1950s and 1960s, DDT and other pesticides were used to kill the tsetse in the wild. This was also very effective, although today we know that DDT can do severe damage to the environment. Pesticides are also used to combat the kissing bugs in South America.

Recently, a new technique has been used that shows great promise of completely wiping out the tsetse in areas where its numbers have already been reduced by other methods. Scientists have discovered that if they expose male tsetse flies to gamma radiation, the flies become sterile (incapable of fertilizing a female's eggs). A female who mates with these sterile males will not be able to produce a larva. Since each female fly mates only once, this means that she will never produce an offspring, thus dramatically reducing the tsetse population.

Thanks to all of these techniques, the number of people infected with sleeping sickness began to fall off sharply during the twentieth century. To many, it seemed that ultimate victory—the complete eradication of sleeping sickness—was around the corner. But in the last decades of the twentieth century, diseases of all kinds began to reappear, some even more deadly than before. Sleeping sickness was no exception.

5

THE FUTURE OF SLEEPING SICKNESS

Wherever armies have marched, diseases have followed along with them. Until very recently, diseases would kill far more people in an army than enemy soldiers ever would. Epidemics were extremely common after any war; for example, in 1919 a flu epidemic swept the globe on the heels of World War I, eventually killing more people of disease than had died in the war.

Since the early 1980s, there has been an erratic civil war in the African nation of Sudan, a former British colony. The northern portion of the country is inhabited by Islamic Arabs who dominate the government of the nation as a whole. In the southern part of the country live Africans who practice traditional religions or Christianity. In response to the northerners' neglect and repression of the south, rebel groups sprang up and now control much of the nation's southern sections. As the war raged, people fled the fighting, leaving their villages and escaping into the wild. Once there, they came into contact with the tsetse fly. Soon, a sleeping sickness epidemic was sweeping through southern Sudan.

Today, after decades of progress, sleeping sickness is once more on the rise. The World Health Organization (WHO) estimates that 300,000 people a year die from it. The problems of war and the impoverished nature of many African nations make this new epidemic difficult to fight. Foreign aid, which is vital for the expensive medicines needed to treat sleeping sickness, is becoming increasingly difficult to find.

One of the great difficulties in treating tropical diseases is that many drug companies are slow to do research into curing these illnesses or even producing existing drugs. Because so many of the countries where these drugs are most desperately needed are impoverished, it is almost impossible for the companies to make any money through research or development. This has brought pharmaceutical companies under criticism from many organizations. Sometimes, however, it is possible for both sides to win: one use of the sleeping sickness drug eflornithine is as a cream that can be used to eliminate unwanted facial hair. Because of this

Richard J. Markham, chief executive officer of pharmaceutical company Aventis Pharma, which has pledged $25 million to the World Health Organization to help combat sleeping sickness in Africa

cream's popularity (and the drug's multiple uses), eflornithine production will increase, and the company that makes it is now searching for methods to donate supplies of it to countries suffering from sleeping sickness epidemics.

Although many tropical diseases affect people far away, we should not overlook their seriousness. Hundreds of thousands of people suffer from sleeping sickness today in Africa. At least 16 million people in Central and South America suffer from Chagas' disease. And schistosomiasis, a disease most people in America have never heard of, affects 200 million people around the world, killing 200,000 of them every year. It is second only to malaria among the parasitical diseases. And it remains a danger in many places that are popular tourist spots, such as Puerto Rico, Saint Lucia, Egypt, and Brazil.

Unlike the early exploration of Africa by Europeans, today people can travel in a matter of hours to almost any spot on the earth. A joyful vacation to Africa or South America may result in a serious infection. Even people with the best precautions and training can become exposed: thirty-two veterans of the Gulf War have been diagnosed with leishmaniasis.

People ignore the dangers of disease at their own peril. Thirty years ago, scientists believed that an ultimate victory over most of the major diseases that had plagued humankind for thousands of years would soon be achieved. One of the worst diseases in history, smallpox, had been completely eradicated. Others, such as tuberculosis, had been fully curable for decades. Attention turned elsewhere, toward curing cancer and rare inherited diseases.

Today, few believe that we can totally destroy any disease. Rather than disappearing, tuberculosis has returned in new forms that are not affected by the existing drug therapies. Strange new and threatening diseases, such as hanta virus infections and Ebola, have emerged. Mad cow disease (Creutzfeldt-Jakob disease), which does not seem to be caused by a virus, bacteria, or parasite, could become a major health threat to people around the world, not to mention costing the beef industry untold millions of dollars in lost income. And finally, one disease, AIDS, has exploded upon the world. It has spread to epidemic proportions in many major cities and is becoming a disaster in Africa nearly on the scale of the Black Death. In today's world, which has become increasingly smaller and smaller as people from every part of the globe mix, we cannot ignore the suffering of people because they are distant. The danger of diseases is everyone's problem and everyone's concern.

GLOSSARY

acute   Disease that has a sudden onset and rises
  quickly to a climax.
antibiotic   Drug that kills bacteria. Antibiotics
  have no effect on viruses.
bacteria   Microscopic parasites that infect living
  hosts and grow inside of them.
chronic   Marked by a long duration or frequent
  occurrences.
epidemic   Outbreak of a disease that infects
  many or most people in a certain area, such
  as a city or country.
host   Person or animal infected with a parasite.
immune system   The body's natural defenses
  against diseases.
nagana   Animal infection or disease caused by
  parasites known as trypanosomes.

parasite   Organism that lives on or inside another
   organism and uses its host to stay alive.
reservoir   Organism in which a parasite lives
   and multiplies.
resistance   Ability of a person to keep from
   catching a disease. With many diseases, once
   a person has caught the disease, he or she
   cannot catch it again.
strain   Specific subtype of any one disease.
trypanosome   Single-celled microscopic parasite
   with whiplike tail that causes sleeping sickness
   and Chagas' disease.
virus   Microscopic parasite, much smaller than
   bacteria. A virus is not "alive" and can
   reproduce only within a living cell.

FOR MORE INFORMATION

In the United States

American Association for World Health
1825 K Street, Suite 1208
Washington, DC 20006
(202) 466-5883
Web site: http://www.aawhworldhealth.org

American Society of Tropical Medicine and Hygiene
60 Revere Drive, Suite 500
Northbrook, IL 60062
(847) 480-9592
Web site: http://www.astmh.org

Centers for Disease Control and Prevention (CDC)
1600 Clifton Road
Atlanta, GA 30333
(404) 639-3534
(800) 311-3435
Web site: http://www.cdc.gov

World Health Organization (WHO)
Regional Office for North America
525 23rd Street NW
Washington, DC 20037
(202) 974-3000
Web site: http://www.who.org

In Canada

Health Canada
Population and Public Health Branch
(formerly Laboratory Centre for Disease Control)
Tunney's Pasture
AL 0913A
Ottawa, ON K1A 0K9
(613) 957-2991
Web site: http://www.hc-sc.gc.ca

Web Sites

Doctors Without Borders
http://www.doctorswithoutborders.org

National Foundation for Infectious Diseases
http://www.nfid.org

Tropical Diseases Collaborating Center
http://www.utmb.edu/pathology/
     tropical_diseases.html

FOR FURTHER READING

Farrell, Jeanette. *Invisible Enemies: Stories of Infectious Disease*. New York: Farrar, Straus & Giroux, 1998.

Giblin, James Cross. *When Plague Strikes*. New York: HarperCollins Publishers, 1995.

Karlen, Arno. *Man and Microbes: Disease and Plagues in History and Modern Times*. New York: Touchtone Books, 1996.

McKelvey, John J., Jr. *Man Against Tsetse: Struggle for Africa*. Ithaca, New York: Cornell University Press, 1973.

McNeill, William H. *Plagues and Peoples*. Rev. ed. New York: Anchor Press, 1998.

INDEX

CREDITS

About the Author

Writer, computer programmer, and poet Fred Ramen lives in New York City. A self-described history nut, he is also the author of *Tuberculosis* and *Influenza,* as well as five other books for the Rosen Publishing Group. Ramen can frequently be seen catching an opera at Lincoln Center, a ball game at Shea Stadium, or a movie at the Film Forum. He was a semi-finalist in the 1997 *Jeopardy!* Tournament of Champions.

Photo Credits

Cover, chapter title interior photos, p. 32 © Oliver Mekes/Photo Researchers; p. 4 © Bettmann/Corbis; p. 8 © Jean Loup Charmet/Science Photo Library; p. 12 © Kevin Schafer/Corbis; p. 16 © David & Peter Turnley/Corbis; p. 18 © Hulton Archive; p. 22 © Lock & Whitfield/Hulton Archive; pp. 24, 35 © Custom Medical Stock Photo; p. 25 © Sinclair Stammers/Science Photo Library; p. 30 © Meckes/Ottowa Photo Researchers; pp. 38, 46 © Mark Edwards/Peter Arnold; pp. 42, 43 © Science Photo Library/Photo Researchers; p. 48 © Nicole Duplaix/Corbis; p. 53 © AP/Wide World Photos.

Series Design

Evelyn Horovicz

Layout

Les Kanturek